Acknowledgements

Educational consultant Viv Edwards, Professor of Language in Education, University of Reading.
Illustrations by Tessa Richardson-Jones.
Photographs by Zul Mukhida except for:
pp. 4t, 13l John Heinrich, p. 13r Tim Richardson, p. 14bl and br John Heinrich, p. 19 Tim Richardson, Zul Colour Library; p. 3 John Birdsall Photography; p. 8b Ben Dallimore/RNIB; p. 16 Shout Pictures; p. 17 Peter Sanders Photography; p. 18 3M United Kingdom plc; p. 20l copyright London Transport Museum; p. 20 centre Sporting Pictures (UK) Ltd; p. 21b BBC Picture Archives.

The author and publisher would like to thank: the staff and pupils of Balfour Infant School, Brighton; Nahib and Kitty; British Telecom plc; RNIB; 3M United Kingdom plc; Simon Hart; Mike King.

A CIP catalogue record for this book is available from the British Library.

ISBN 0-7136-4244-0

First published 1995 by A&C Black (Publishers) Ltd
35 Bedford Row, London WC1R 4JH

Typeset in 15/21pt Univers Medium by
Rowland Phototypesetting Ltd, Bury St Edmunds, Suffolk.

Printed in France by Partenaires

Keeping in touch

Nicola Edwards

A&C Black · London

We can send messages
by speaking to
each other . . .

. . . or by using
sign language.

Some people write down what they want to say.

The message can be for one person

or a special group of people

or for everyone.

If you don't want everyone to read what you have written, you can send a secret message.

This message is in back-to-front mirror writing. The girl is holding the message up to the mirror to read it. Can you see what it says?

This boy is writing his message in lemon juice instead of ink. You cannot see what he is writing because the lemon juice is so pale.

His friend will be able to read the writing by heating the paper until the lemon juice turns brown.

Have you ever sent a secret message?

People often write letters to each other.

This girl is not very well. She has received a letter from her doctor, asking her to visit the hospital for a check-up.

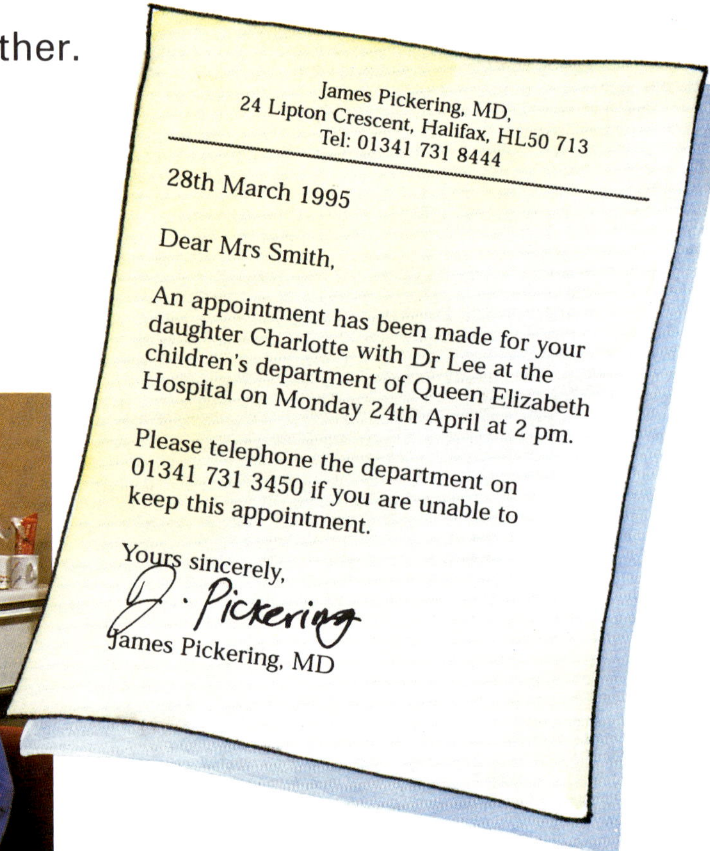

James Pickering, MD,
24 Lipton Crescent, Halifax, HL50 713
Tel: 01341 731 8444

28th March 1995

Dear Mrs Smith,

An appointment has been made for your daughter Charlotte with Dr Lee at the children's department of Queen Elizabeth Hospital on Monday 24th April at 2 pm.

Please telephone the department on 01341 731 3450 if you are unable to keep this appointment.

Yours sincerely,

J. Pickering

James Pickering, MD

This blind person has been sent a letter which has been typed in Braille. The Braille alphabet is made up of a pattern of raised dots on paper. He is reading the letter by running his fingers over the dots.

Kate and Nicola have a granny who lives in Canada. They have sent her a letter telling her all their news. What else have they sent to help her keep in touch with what they've been doing?

Dear Granny,
It was lovely to speak to you on the phone last week.
We're sending you a video of Jane's wedding so that you can see us being her bridesmaids.

At school on Tuesday we took part in a sponsored aerobics session to raise money for the drama club - we were even in the local paper!

Uncle Michael brought Sara to see us at the weekend - we all went to a zoo, a funfair and an animal park. Before they left we made a tape for you so that you can hear all of us singing 'Happy Birthday' to you.

Lots of love,

Nicola and Kate xxx

People often keep in touch with each other at special times of the year.

Have you ever had a postcard from someone on holiday?

Or a Christmas card?

Or an invitation to a birthday party?

This letter is ready to be posted.
The stamp on the envelope tells you whether the letter is going first or second class.

The address tells you where the letter is going.

This boy is posting the letter in a postbox.

The sign on the postbox tells him what time the letter will be collected.

This is what the envelope looks like after it has been delivered. How is it different? What new messages can you see?

People often keep in touch by talking to each other on the telephone.

The boy below wants to make a call from a public telephone. The sign on the wall shows him what to do.

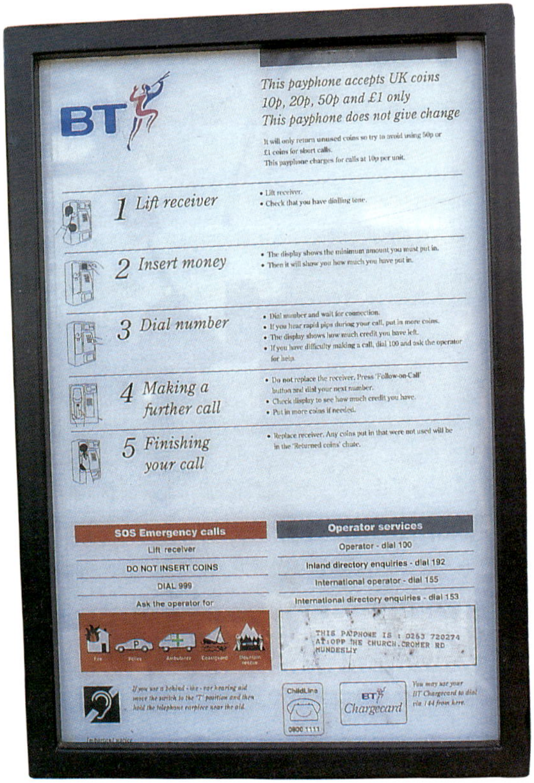

A fax machine is a special sort of telephone. It can send and receive messages written down on paper.

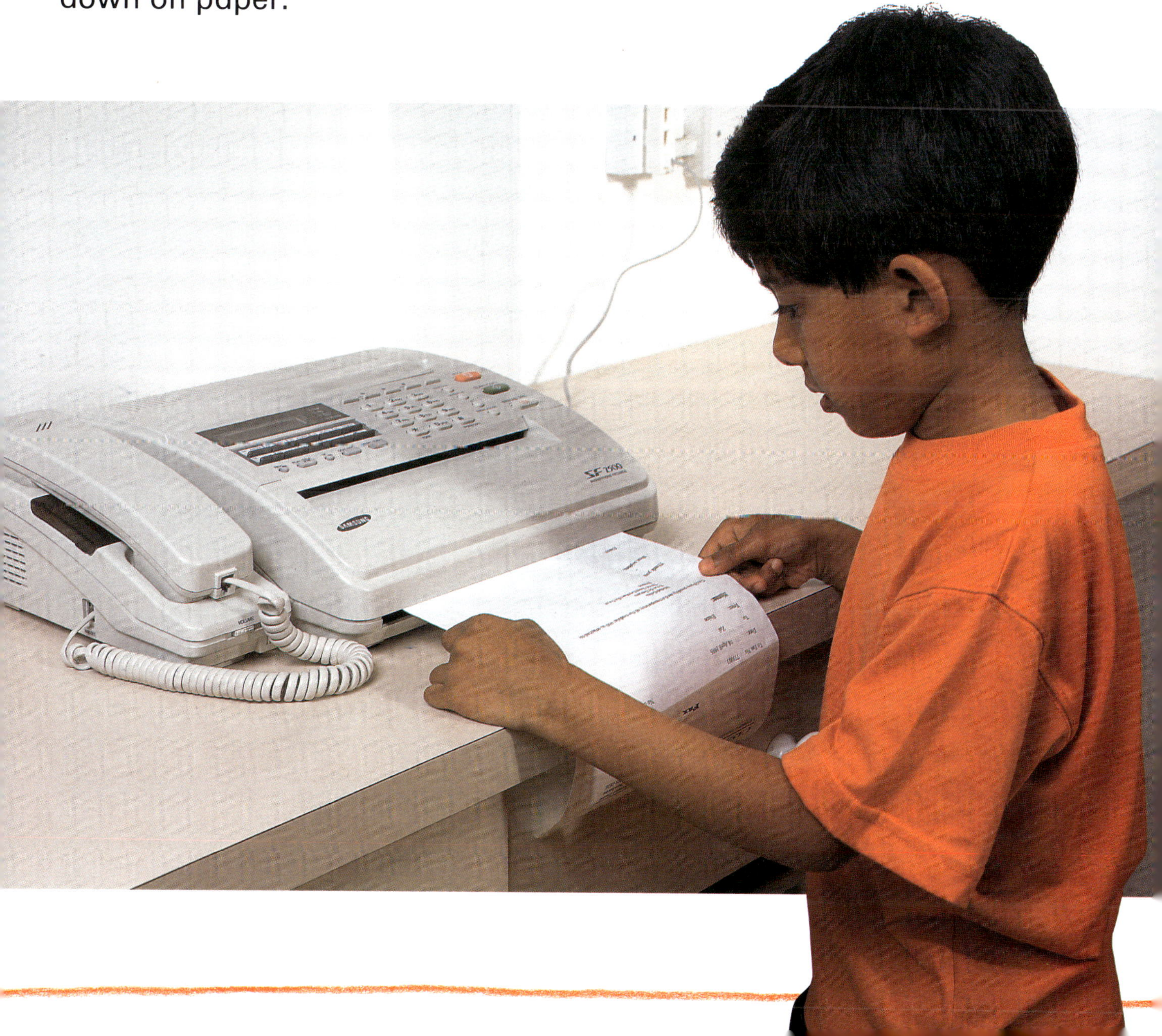

Sometimes lots of people need to hear a message at the same time.

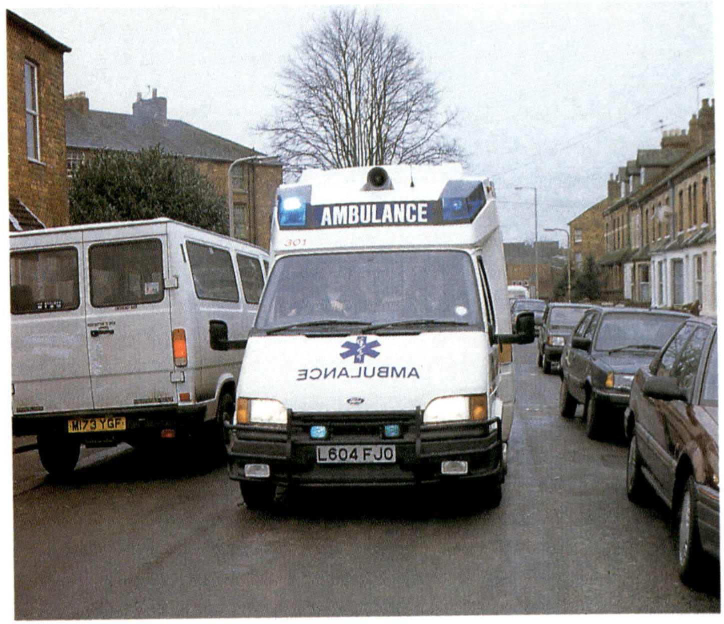

Ambulances need to take ill people to hospital as quickly as possible.
The loud siren and flashing light on this ambulance warn people to keep out of the way as it is in a hurry.

This policeman is talking through a loud hailer to the crowd at a football ground. It makes the sound of his voice louder so that the people at the back of the crowd can hear him.

At this mosque, the voice of the imam, or leader, is played to call the people to prayer.

Sometimes messages are meant for everyone to see.

The flag on this beach warns people that it is not safe to swim in the sea.

This cyclist is wearing special bright clothing so that drivers can see him in the dark.

What do you think these signs are telling the visitors to this building?

There are different ways of finding out about things that are happening all over the world.

How could you find out the result of a tennis match at Wimbledon?

You could go there yourself and watch the match . . .

or listen to it on the radio . . .

or watch it on television . . .

or read about it in a newspaper.

People all over the world are using computers connected by telephone lines to keep in touch with each other.

These children in Manchester are typing messages about themselves and their school on to a computer screen. The computer will send the information along a telephone line to a school in New York in the United States.

The children in New York will send back information about their lives and describe their school to the children in Manchester.

This scientist lives in Cape Town in South Africa. She is using her computer to discuss her ideas with other scientists who are working in Dakar in Senegal and Buenos Aires in Argentina.

Index

For parents and teachers

The aim of the *Messages* series is to help build confidence in children who are just beginning to read, by encouraging them to make meaning from the different kinds of signs and symbols which surround them in their everyday lives. Here are some suggestions for follow-up activities which extend the ideas introduced in the book.

Pages 2/3 Ask the children to think about the different people they speak to during a typical day at home or at school. For example, how do the spoken or signed messages they give and receive help them to decide what they eat during the day? What would they say to make a new person feel welcome at school and what questions would they ask to find out about that person?

Pages 4/5 Take the children on a walk around the school or local area and make a list of the different kinds of written messages which they notice around them. The children could bring in examples of messages in other languages – for example, in newspapers and magazines, on food packaging or in letters from relatives.

Pages 6/7 The children could practise some mirror writing. Provide a guide showing the letters of the alphabet as they appear when written backwards; once they've written their messages, show them how to hold the piece of paper up to a mirror and copy out the reflected messages on to a second piece of paper. You could introduce older children to simple codes as a means of sending secret messages. For more information and ideas for activities see WRITE AWAY by Viv Edwards, published by A & C Black.

Pages 8/9 Make a collection of letters, some of which the children could bring in from home, which have been written for different purposes. What clues can the children find which help them to work out how formal and informal letters differ from each other in terms of, for example, layout, vocabulary and whether they are handwritten or typed? You could take the children to visit the school secretary to see how different types of correspondence are dealt with. Older children could try writing their own letters to relatives or friends.

Pages 10/11 Ask the children to bring in cards their family has received at different times of the year, for example to celebrate a religious festival such as Eid or Diwali, Easter or Christmas, an invitation to a wedding or birthday party, or a holiday postcard. You could use these to illustrate a 'keeping in touch throughout the year' calendar for a wall display. The children could make their own postcards, decorating them with illustrations cut from magazines or travel brochures.

Pages 12/13 Make a collection of stamps from different countries and ask the children to identify the messages on each one, such as country of origin, price and currency, whether the stamp is commemorating a special event and so on. Trace the journey of a letter from sender to recipient and explain how including the postcode (in which each letter and number stands for part of an address) on an addressed envelope can help to speed up this process. Can the children find out the postcode of the school or their home?

Pages 14/15 The school may have a mobile phone or a fax machine which you could show to the children. Ask them to think of some situations in which a mobile phone would be particularly useful. When would it be more suitable to use a fax machine rather than the postal service to send a letter?

Pages 16/17 You could make a tape of different sound signals and ask the children to give the context of each. The selection could include not only 'warning' signals, for example a car alarm or train hooter, but also those which summon people or call attention, such as church bells, a referee's whistle or the school bell.

Pages 18/19 Take the children on a walk around the local area. Make a list of the different visual messages they notice, such as traffic lights changing colour, road markings and signs in shop windows.

Pages 20/21 You could invite a journalist from your local paper into school to talk to the children about how news is gathered and communicated. The children could then make their own newspaper, using stories, photographs and drawings to describe the events of their week. You could discuss how events in a nursery story such as the tortoise and the hare would be reported in different media, for example, interviews with the participants, film of a commentary on the race itself and the reactions of spectators.

Pages 22/23 If your school has a computer which is linked to the e-mail network, the children could contact a school in another country to exchange information and ideas. Which country would the children like to find out about? What questions would they ask to find out how the children they make contact with spend their day, at home and at school?